"I'D LIKE TO DEDICATE THIS BOOK TO GOD, MY WIFE LIZZIE, AND DEAR FATHERS IN CHRIST, WHO HAVE ALWAYS LOVED AND BELIEVED IN ME." JASON

"TO MY WIFE HANNAH, AS AN ALTERNATIVE TO CHEESY CHRISTMAS MOVIES." DAN

First published in 2022 by Bridge Church Publishing

Text © Jason Rogers 2021
Illustrations © Dan Jones 2022

Printed in the United Kingdom by Bookprinting UK
ISBN 978-1-7391872-0-0

The rights of Jason Rogers to be identified as the author and Dan Jones to be identified as the illustrator have been asserted by them in accordance with the Copyright, Design and Patents Act 1988

Typography: White Wood, Swistblnk Monthoers, Arial

A CIP catalogue record for this book is available from the British Library

For news and future projects, or to get in touch, visit:
www.anchor-lines.com/books

WE WOULD ALSO LIKE TO SAY A HUGE THANK YOU TO THE BRIDGE CHURCH, ST. IVES, WHO HAD FAITH FOR THIS PROJECT, AND TO STEFAN LISTON, WHO HAS INSPIRED US ALL BY HIS POEM 'HE WAS AND IS AND IS TO COME'.

WAS IT QUIET, CALM AND PEACEFUL?

WAS IT BUSY WITH LOTS OF PEOPLE?

WERE THERE ANIMALS ALL AROUND?

DID MARY GIVE BIRTH ON THE GROUND?

OR WAS SHE LAYING ON A TABLE?

AND WAS IT REALLY IN A STABLE?

WAS THERE JOY AND SOUNDS OF LAUGHTER?

OR DID IT FEEL LIKE A DISASTER?

BUT FOR MARY AND JOSEPH, SOMEWHERE TO STAY

AND FOR BABY, A MANGER, WITH A MATTRESS OF HAY

IT WAS NOTHING LIKE THEY HAD EXPECTED

HARDLY THE PLAN THEY HAD PERFECTED

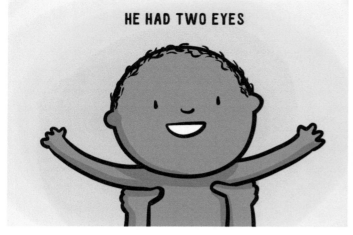

HE HAD TWO EYES

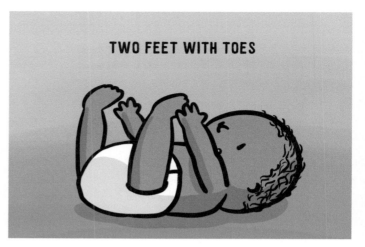

TWO FEET WITH TOES

MADE SMELLS THAT
MADE YOU
PINCH YOUR NOSE!

A NORMAL BABY LIKE ANY OTHER

VULNERABLE, SMALL,
HELD CLOSE BY HIS MOTHER

THE NAME

THAT WOULD LIVE ON FOREVER, IMMORTAL IN FAME

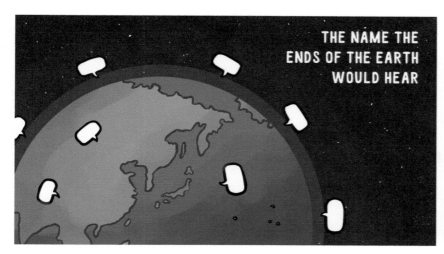

THE NAME THE ENDS OF THE EARTH WOULD HEAR

THE NAME THAT WOULD STIR UP JOY

AND FEAR

SUCH POWER TO CHANGE ENTIRE NATIONS

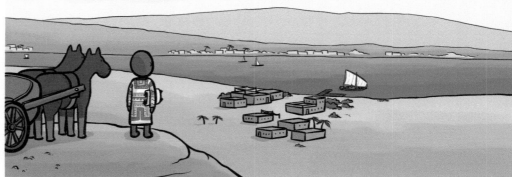

THE NAME THAT WOULD TOUCH THE GENERATIONS

BUT FOR NOW A BABY

A CHILD

A SON

AND A MUM AND DAD WITH THEIR LITTLE ONE

BUT WHATEVER WAS HAPPENING WAS INTERRUPTED

BY SOME VISITORS ARRIVING QUITE UNEXPECTED

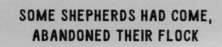

SOME SHEPHERDS HAD COME, ABANDONED THEIR FLOCK

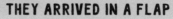

THEY ARRIVED IN A FLAP

THEY WERE IN SHOCK

WITH A MESSAGE WHICH FRANKLY COULD NOT BE STRANGER, ABOUT THIS BABY IN THE MANGER

THEY SAID THIS BABY WAS NOT NORMAL AT ALL

AN ANGEL TOLD THEM THAT THOUGH HE WAS SMALL

THIS JESUS WAS THE KING OF KINGS

GOD THE MAKER OF ALL THINGS

THE ONE WHO MADE THE SUN...

...AND MOON

THE ONE WHO MADE THE MONTH OF JUNE

THE ONE WHO MADE THE BUGS AND BEES

THE ONE WHO MADE THE PLANTS AND TREES

THE ONE WHO GAVE THE BIRDS THEIR FLIGHT

THE ONE WHO GAVE THE HILLS THEIR HEIGHT

THE ONE WHO GAVE THE SEA ITS DEPTH

THE ONE WHO GAVE THE DESERTS THEIR BREADTH

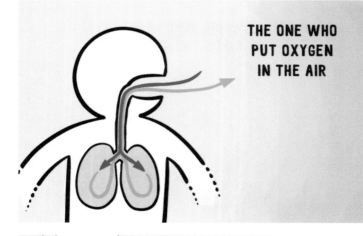
THE ONE WHO PUT OXYGEN IN THE AIR

THE ONE WHO GAVE FIRE ITS FLARE

THE ONE WHO BRINGS US RAIN AND SNOW

WHO MADE THE PLANETS LONG AGO

THE GOD WHO MADE THE GALAXY

BUT MOST PRECIOUS OF ALL, YOU AND ME

HOW COULD IT BE TRUE?
THIS SEEMS SO ODD!

THAT THIS BABY COULD
IN FACT BE GOD?

BUT THE SHEPHERD'S MESSAGE
WAS NOT WRONG

THIS WAS GOD'S PLAN ALL ALONG

THAT
GOD
WOULD COME
IN HUMAN FORM,

THE NIGHT THAT
JESUS CHRIST
WAS BORN.

WHEN THE SON OF GOD FROM HEAVEN CAME DOWN

HE LEFT BEHIND HIS GOLDEN CROWN

HIS GLORY AND SPLENDOUR HE LEFT BEHIND

AND CAME TO EARTH TO HEAL THE BLIND

TO CURE THE SICK

TO SERVE THE POOR

TO PICK UP PEOPLE OFF THE FLOOR

TO RAISE UP PEOPLE FROM THE DEAD

THAT THEY WOULD HAVE NEW LIFE INSTEAD

TO CARE FOR THOSE WHO COULDN'T COPE

TO PREACH GOOD NEWS OF GRACE

AND LOVE

THAT HE WAS THE SON OF GOD ABOVE

THAT HE WAS THE ONE THEY WERE WAITING FOR

HE HADN'T COME AS A GOD OF WAR

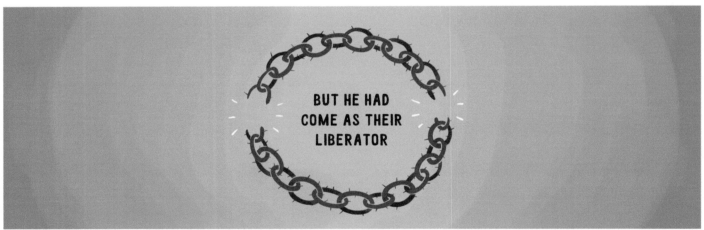

BUT HE HAD COME AS THEIR LIBERATOR

THE SHEPHERDS SAID HE WAS OUR SAVIOUR

THE NIGHT GOD CAME TO SAVE US ALL

THE NIGHT THAT JESUS CHRIST WAS BORN

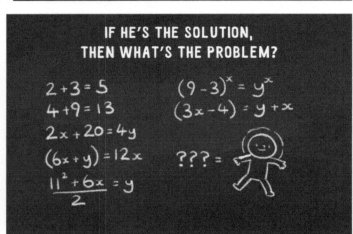

IMAGINE FOR A MOMENT THE PERFECT DAD

HE TAUGHT YOU EVERYTHING, GOOD FROM BAD

HE KEPT YOU WARM
AND KEPT YOU FED

TOOK THE TIME TO TUCK YOU INTO BED

HELD YOU CLOSE AND KEPT YOU SAFE,
SAID YOU'D ALWAYS HAVE A PLACE

HE GAVE YOU
JOYFUL WORK TO DO

MADE A WHOLE WORLD JUST FOR YOU

AND THE ONLY THING HE ASKS
FROM YOU IS TO TRUST HIM

AND LOVE HIM AS HE LOVES YOU

BUT WHAT HAPPENED NEXT
WASN'T HAPPY AT ALL

WHAT HAPPENED NEXT
WE CALL "THE FALL"

THAT REBELLIOUS
SPIRIT HAD ENTERED IN

TO THE HEART OF MAN,
A HEART OF SIN

AND THEN THEY COULD NO LONGER STAND,
WITH GOD THE FATHER, THEIR LOVING DAD

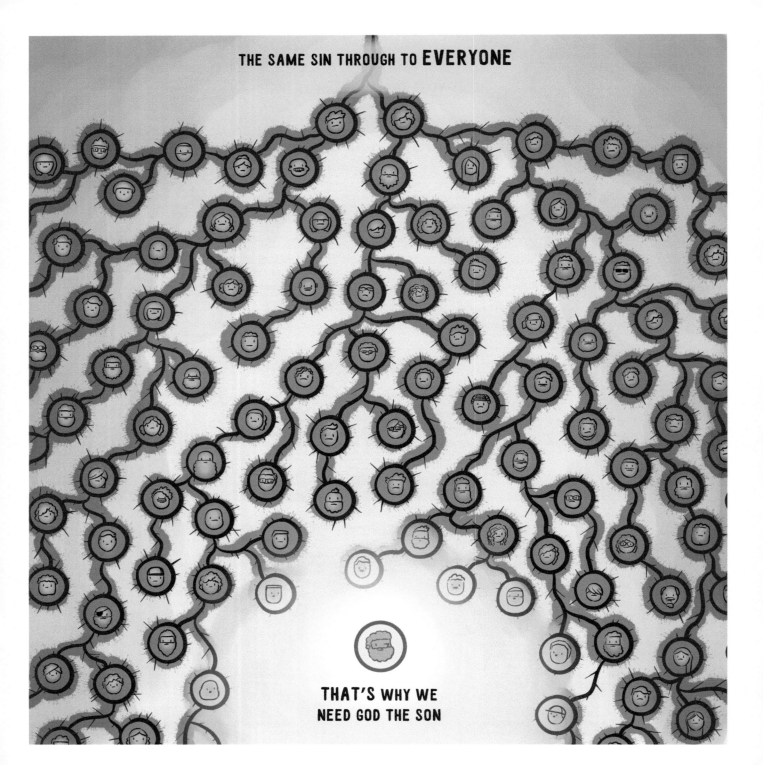

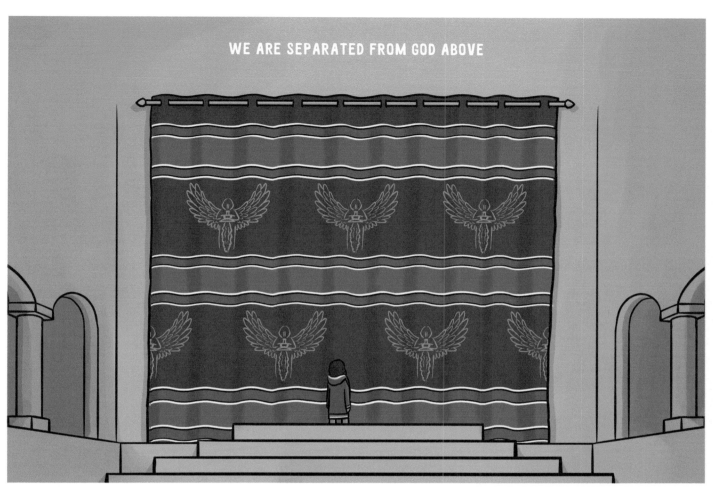

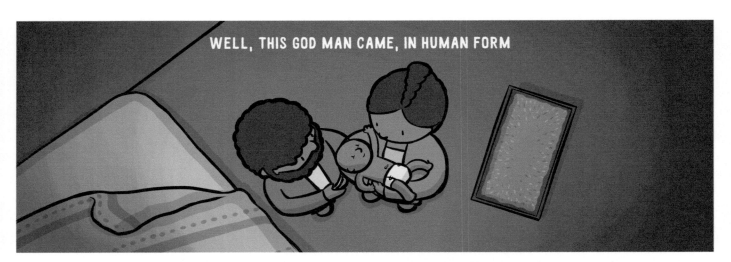

THIS BABY GREW UP, LIVED A NORMAL LIFE

WITH LAUGHTER

JOY

FEAR

AND STRIFE

IT WAS AROUND THIRTY YEARS OF AGE,
THAT JESUS' LIFE BEGAN A NEW STAGE

HE BEGAN TO DO ALL
THE WORK AND MORE,
THAT I TOLD YOU ABOUT
IN THE SECTION BEFORE

THEN AFTER JUST A FEW SHORT YEARS,
HIS JOURNEY SHIFTED UP A FEW GEARS

'THE ONLY WAY YOU'LL BE SAVED MY BROTHERS,
IS IF I GIVE MY LIFE FOR THE SAKE OF ALL OTHERS'

THIS IS THE REASON
HE WAS BORN

TO BRING US LIFE

AND HEARTS TRANSFORM

TO BRING US BACK TO OUR LOVING FATHER,
THAT WE WOULD LIVE HAPPILY EVER AFTER

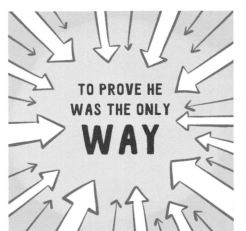

HE CAME TO EARTH ON A MISSION
TO SAVE MANKIND FROM THEIR CONDITION

AND EVEN WHEN HE WAS JUST A BABE,
HIS MISSION WAS ALWAYS TO COME AND SAVE

THE SAVING WORK WAS
AS GOOD AS DONE

THE FIGHT FOR US WAS
AS GOOD AS WON

THE DIVIDING CURTAIN AS GOOD AS TORN

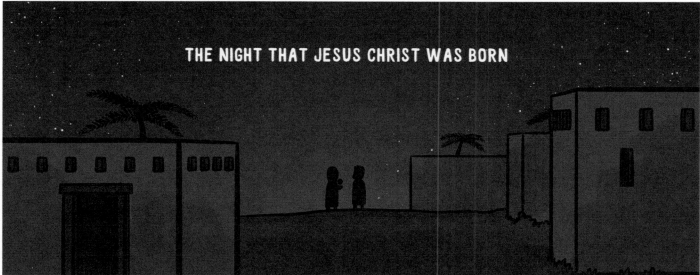

THE NIGHT THAT JESUS CHRIST WAS BORN

NOW THERE'S ONLY ONE THING LEFT TO SAY

WHAT DOES THIS MEAN FOR CHRISTMAS DAY?

PERHAPS A TIME OF FESTIVE CHEER

SURROUNDED BY THOSE YOU HOLD MOST DEAR

FAMILY, FOOD, FRIENDS, AND FUN

PRESENTS AND STOCKINGS, THE LIST GOES ON

OR PERHAPS A TIME OF SADNESS

AND YOU STRUGGLE TO FIND THAT HEART OF GLADNESS

MEMORIES OF CHRISTMAS'S PAST

OF PROMISES WHICH DIDN'T LAST

THE BITING PAIN OF LOVED ONES LOST

OR JUST THE STRUGGLE TO MEET THE COST

WHATEVER IS ON YOUR HEART THIS YEAR,
REMEMBER THE NIGHT THAT HE CAME HERE

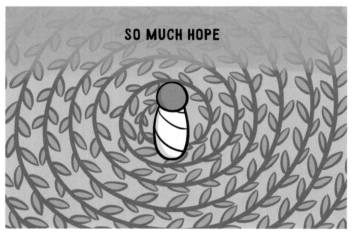

SO MUCH HOPE

IN SUCH A SMALL THING

THE PROMISE THAT WE CAN KNOW OUR KING

THIS CHRISTMAS
WHATEVER IS IN YOUR HOME,
KNOW THAT YOU
ARE NEVER ALONE

KNOW THAT YOU HAVE A FATHER ABOVE,
WHO LONGS TO COME AND SHOW YOU LOVE

HIS VALUE AND WORTH
YOU CANNOT MEASURE

HE CAME TO GIVE
YOU THE GREATEST
TREASURE

NEW LIFE, WITH HIM, FOREVERMORE

THE NIGHT THAT JESUS CHRIST WAS BORN